Ysaye, Kreisler, Wilhelmj, Huberman, Kubelik, Thibaud.

F. C. Schang is a native of Manhattan Island, a New Yorker born, bred and educated there, graduate of the Columbia University School of Journalism, Class of 1915, for a few years reporter on the New York Tribune, and then for half a century manager of concert artists and attractions.

In the course of these duties he was at various times involved in the management of numerous violinists, among them Mischa Elman, Jacques Thibaud, Albert Spalding, Toscha Seidel, Robert Virovai, Erica Morini, Bronislaw Huberman, Ruggiero Ricci, Carroll Glenn, Tossy Spivakovsky, Henri Temianka, Syzman Goldberg, Ma Si-Hon and David Oistrakh.

Owner of a great collection of visiting cards, in 1971 he published a book entitled *Visiting Cards of Celebrities* which was favorably received. In 1973 he published an off-shoot of this big book called *Visiting Cards of Prima Donnas*. This current volume is a second off-shoot, showing the cards of some 25 odd violin virtuosos, their photographs, and bright comment on their doings.

VISITING CARDS

of

VIOLINISTS

from the

COLLECTION

of

F. C. SCHANG

with comment by him

JOSEPH
PATELSON MUSIC HOUSE

NEW YORK, N. Y.

The cards and photographs shown from the author's collections unless otherwise indicated.

THANKS

Thanks are due to those who assisted as follows: Gerald William Burg, Theodor Bera, Yvonne de Castro, William Judd, Edward N. Waters, Rudolf Firkusny, Oscar Shapiro, Mary Jane Schang, Vitya Babin and Neva Garner Greenwood.

Copyright assigned 1979 to
Joseph Patelson d/b/d
Joseph Patelson Music House, New York City
160 West 56 Street, New York, N.Y. 10019

International Standard Book Number: 0-915282-05-4
Library of Congress Card Number: 79-63411

Printed in the United States of America
by Southeastern Printing Company
Stuart, Florida

ALPHABETICAL ROSTER

of

VIOLINISTS

INTRODUCTION

THE SOUND of the violin being most like the human voice, it is not surprising that it is the favorite musical instrument of the western world. Moreover, of all musical instruments devised by man, the violin is capable of the most exalted song.

It is also the cornerstone of the symphony orchestra, and the violin family supplies the body of tone which makes this great ensemble the most noble of all musical manifestations.

Many years were to pass before the violins of the great Cremona craftsmen were to be exploited as solo instruments. To be sure, great artists such as Corelli, Tartini, Viotti have left compositions which reveal that they expected and required technical virtuosity from executants of their pieces.

About 1720 J. S. Bach, noted as a composer of church cantatas and large works for the organ, nevertheless found occasion to compose six works for unaccompanied violin. The 4th of these, a partita in D minor, contains the celebrated Chaconne, a monumental challenge to virtuosity and musicianship which remains to this day a marvel of polyphonal complexity. Given ideal conditions — a master violin, a master to play it, a rapt and knowing audience — this Chaconne may realize the highest possibilities of musical experience.

But it was Paganini who really launched the violin as a solo instrument. He was the trail-blazer who demonstrated that the public would pay real money to hear a violin virtuoso and that it was possible to earn a fortune in this field.

So since his day there has been a steady succession of violin virtuosos bidding for the favor of the public. Most of these players are listed in this volume, which came about because it was disclosed that all of them used visiting cards, such cards being a necessity to folks whose livelihoods depended on social contacts.

The author's comprehensive book *Visiting Cards of Celebrities* published in 1971 contained the cards of a dozen violinists, most of them with sparse information and no pictures. To show the cards of violinists, many with interesting messages, to reveal what these people looked like, and to amplify former scant coverage, is the purpose of this book.

Eigenth.u.Verl.v.G.Fiorini, München.   Heliogravüre Obernetter, München.

NICOLO PAGANINI
(1782-1840)

There being no recordings of Paganini's playing, an appraisal of this artist's work must depend on an examination of criticisms, tracts, articles and books, of which there exist a huge number. A judicious distillation of some of this material establishes that Paganini was the greatest violinist up to and including his own era, and perhaps the greatest ever.

One statement cannot be challenged: Paganini was certainly the greatest showman ever to play the violin. His gaunt visage, his wild looks and his eccentric behavior on the stage were all part of an act to make the impossible effects produced on his instrument seem supernatural.

These impressions were heightened by his choice of program material, mostly variations on themes from operas, which, because he was the first fiddler to dispense with printed music, seemed to be improvisations. In the middle of a piece, he might break a string or two and continue as if nothing had happened. Again, a number of his pet selections were advertised to be played on "one string, the fourth string", a stunt supposed to require unearthly powers possessed only by him.

Il Cavaliere Nicolo Paganini

Virtuoso di Camera di S. M.

L'IMPERATORE D'AUSTRIA

e primo maestro di Concerto di

S. M. il' RE di PRUSSIA

This fourth string of the violin is the G string, but never so called by Paganini, as he tuned it up half a tone, sometimes a whole tone, sometimes just "up," to secure the eerie effects of which he was a unique master. Paganini habitually tuned his instrument up a half-tone when playing with orchestral accompaniment. For solo work he employed thin strings and a low bridge to produce his peculiar brand of weird harmonics, hitherto unheard in the concert hall.

In addition to fantastic pyrotechnics, it was sometimes Paganini's mood to imitate bird calls, and sounds of the nursery and barnyard. This kind of clap-trap astonished the uncultured, but displeased others, and occasionally got him a scorching review.

Notwithstanding all this folderol which made him the greatest drawing card in Europe, Paganini was heard and applauded by serious musicians such as Liszt and Schumann. These two, together with Brahms, recognized that Paganini's Opus 1, *24 Caprices for Violin Alone,* was a masterpiece, and they borrowed themes for their own compositions. This great work of Paganini is an exhaustive exposition of the treasures stored in a violin, and a major contribution to violin literature which all violinists must study.

Paganini never visited America. In fact he never left Italy until he was 46 years of age. His first trip was to

Vienna, accompanied by the soprano Antonia Bianchi, who was his assisting artist and the mother of his three-year-old son, Achille. Phenomenal success attended him there and in other European countries until illness terminated his tours two years before his death.

Paganini was enamoured of decorations, medals, gifts from royalty and similar distinctions. It is therefore not surprising that his visiting cards play up his titles and honors. On the first card which is raspberry in color and has an embossed border, "Le Baron N. Paganini, Commandeur et Chevalier de plusieurs Ordres," he does not deign to enumerate them, doubtless because there are too many to list on a card; but on the second card, which deals with royalty, he is particular to specify that he is Court Virtuoso to His Majesty the Emperor of Austria, and Master Recitalist to His Majesty the King of Prussia.

While it is often considered that Paganini was the greatest violinist of all time, two factors are influencing present day judgment. For one thing, no current violinist would consider the sort of program offered by Paganini. And for another, since his day the violin literature has been greatly augmented. A modern fiddler has to know what Paganini knew, and in addition thereto important contributions by Vieuxtemps, Wieniawski, Sarasate, Lalo, Mendelssohn, Brahms, Tschaikowsky, Bruch, Kreisler, Saint-Saens, Bartok, Shostakovitch and many others.

OLE BULL (1810-1880)

"I had a very pleasant party-kin last night in Cambridge at the Longfellow's where there was a mad-cap fiddler, Ole Bull, who played wonderfully on his instrument and charmed me still more by his oddities and character."

Extract from a letter of Thackeray (Dec. 1855)

During the first half of last century, when American listeners to music were generally unsophisticated, it was their good fortune to meet up with Ole Bull, a Norwegian violinist whose playing catered to the taste of a young country.

At that time violin recitals as performed today were unknown. It was taken for granted that one artist could not hold the attention of an audience for a two-hour stretch. Concerts were in fact *concerted,* with a number of artists participating.

Ole Bull was a big likeable fellow with blond hair, bright blue eyes and a magnetic personality. People liked him before he lifted his bow. And after he played they liked him even more, for he did not tax them with difficult music, but preferred to entertain them with simple pieces and improvisations, often on themes he might ask them to suggest. Playing this kind of fare his technique seemed prodigious and he was a very great success.

Between 1843 and 1870 Bull made many tours of the U.S. His first tour lasted two years during which he played 200 concerts. In this period American scenery inspired two popular numbers, *Niagara* and *The Solitude of the Prairies.*

Nine years later in 1852 he returned to head a concert company organized by Maurice Strakosch to introduce his eight-year-old sister-in-law, Adelina Patti. At this time the public was still talking about the clean-up made by Jenny

PROGRAMME

—— FOR ——

OLE BULL'S

GRAND CONCERT,

—— ON ——

TUESDAY EVENING, OCTOBER 4, 1853,

—— AT THE ——

NEW MUSIC HALL,

ON WHICH OCCASION HE WILL BE ASSISTED BY

SIG'NA ADELINA PATTI,

THE MUSICAL PHENOMENON,

—— AND ——

MAURICE STRAKOSCH,

THE GREAT PIANIST, DIRECTOR AND CONDUCTOR.

Price of Admission, One Dollar.

☞ SEATS may be secured at Mr. E. H. WADE's MUSIC STORE, 197 Washington Street. ☜

DOORS OPEN AT 7. CONCERT TO COMMENCE AT 8 O'CLOCK.

☞ MR. STRAKOSCH will perform on a splendid GRAND 7 OCTAVE PIANOFORTE, from Chickering's celebrated manufactory.

Dutton & Wentworth, Printers, 37 Congress Street, Boston.

Lind, the Swedish nightingale who had left America the year before (1851) with a big fortune in dollars, over 300,000 of the same. Strakosch wanted to follow up on Lind's vogue. History notes that in picking young Adelina as a future star he was very right. She became the greatest singer of her day, the most *prima* of the *donnas*.

With Ole Bull as a headliner and the child Patti as a debutante, the concert company was a great success. Bull played four selections: two of his own, *A Mother's Prayer* and *Variations on Yankee Doodle;* and two by Paganini: *A Carnival of Venice,* and *Le Streghe,* comic Witches' Dance, a set of variations for "the fourth string". Standing on the table shown, Adelina sang airs from *Sonnambula* and *Linda di Chamounix, Comin' thro' the Rye,* and Jenny Lind's *Echo Song.*

From the Museum of the City of New York, Theatre and Music Collection

As the tour concluded Bull decided to put in effect a grandiose notion of starting a Norwegian colony in the U.S.A. He bought a tract of 12,000 acres in Pennsylvania for this purpose, but alas! the title proved faulty, the project involved unforeseen costs beyond his means and he was obliged to withdraw, having lost a fortune.

On his final swing around the circuit in 1870 he met in Madison, Wis., the lady who became his second wife, an American named Sara Thorpe. His last ten years were spent in his beloved homeland, with occasional short jaunts to Europe and one to Egypt. Although then 66 years of age he was still game for a press stunt, and played a concert on top of the Cheops pyramid. This gambit paid off and his concert the next day was to a crowded house.

HENRY VIEUXTEMPS (1820-1881)

This fine Belgian had the benefit of a great teacher in his youth, Charles de Bériot, himself an excellent player and the husband of Maria Malibran, celebrated singer. The younger sister of Malibran was another famous singer, Pauline Viardot, friend of de Musset, Berlioz, Gounod, Meyerbeer, Chopin, Liszt, the Schumanns, Brahms and the writer Turgenev.

With the well-connected Bériot to sponsor him, Vieuxtemps had entrée to the musical intelligentsia of this day, and with his own talent and graces he easily made the grade.

In the midst of busy European tours, Vieuxtemps had occasion to visit America three times, in 1844, 1857 and 1870. On his first trip as a young man of 24, a New York reviewer remarked that he wore gold earrings, and that his sister who played his accompaniments was a very pretty girl. The second tour was with the pianist Thalberg and the last one with Christine Nilssen, the soprano who later opened the Metropolitan Opera House, New York, singing the lead in *Faust*.

Vieuxtemps was an important composer of violin music. His six concertos are all standard in the violin repertory, and several of them are often played by current performers. The sixth was dedicated to the violinist Wilma Norman-Noruda (later Lady Hallé) and first played by her.

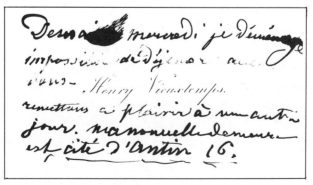

The above card, considered rare, is a removal notice — new address is Cité d'Antin 16.

16

In his latter years while heading the violin department at the Brussels Conservatory, he was forced to quit because of a paralytic stroke. Seeking warmer climes, he retired to Algeria, and there met with an unusual death. Riding in a carriage, a crazed Arab, complete stranger, threw a stone which hit him causing a mortal injury.

JOSEPH JOACHIM

(1831-1907)

During the latter half of his life Joseph Joachim was the most famous violinist in Europe and occupied a position in the musical world which has no counterpart today. He was a kind of oracle before whom professional string players appeared with problems in Higher Musicianship. Joachim's monumental reputation and learning permitted answers which were accepted as final.

In particular, should a player be in doubt about any phase of the Beethoven, Brahms or Bruch (G minor) concertos, Joachim was the Supreme Court on these. Should a group of quartet players strike a road block in rehearsal, then Joachim, founder and first violin of the prestigious Joachim Quartet, was able to quickly set them on the right track.

This man's position as an arbiter was further enhanced by the fact that for more than 30 years he was head of the Berlin Hochschule for Music, an admirable vantage point from which to disseminate wisdom. On the faculty with him as leader of the composition department was Prof. Dr. Max Bruch, composer himself of four violin concertos, the greatest of which referred to above was dedicated to Joachim.

Other musicians of international repute who were close friends were Mendelssohn, Liszt, Clara Schumann and Brahms. The latter was indeed Joachim's best friend, as these two men lived on the same musical street and vibrated on the same wave length. For many years Brahms submitted his compositions to Joachim for inspection and comment before sending them to his publisher. Joachim was of inestimable value to Brahms in the composition of his great violin concerto, wrote the cadenza for it and it was dedicated to him.

Joachim - Quartett.

This great friendship was terminated in 1880 when Joachim divorced his wife, a concert contralto whose maiden name was Amalie Weiss. Brahms admired Mrs. Joachim who had often been a charming hostess to his visits, and his partisanship of her offended Joachim. (Cause of the marital rift was said to have been professional jealousy!)

> Dear Mr. Gordon, I am afraid
> I shall not be able to come
> tomorrow to the Concert,
> Joseph Joachim
> but I hope I may hear your
> friend on Wednesday, when
> you come and he feels inclined
> Berlin to bring his Violin Kurfürstendamm 217.

The card above refers to the first violin recital in Berlin by the young American violinist Albert Spalding, then 19 years of age. Accompanying Spalding was a London friend and patron of music, Henry Evans Gordon. This gentleman was also a friend of Joachim, and he expected to get Joachim to attend Spalding's recital.

Joachim was unable to do so, but he did receive Spalding at his school the day following, heard him play, and gave him some pointers on the Bruch concerto. The year was 1907 . . . the veteran musician was in his 76th year and was to die several months later.

The 100th anniversary of the founding of the prestigious Berlin *Hochschule für Musik* was in 1969, and this memorial stamp depicts Joachim as a young man.

HENRI WIENIAWSKI
(1835-1880)

Following Vieuxtemps and Joachim, both of whom greatly esteemed him, the Polish virtuoso-composer Wieniawski had a world-wide reputation. He was frequently consulted by composers of works for the violin who sought his judgment on the playability of their creations.

This artist was a heavy drinker and a compulsive gambler. He several times was obliged to sell or pawn named violins to bail out of gambling losses. Nowadays the loss of a costly instrument might put a fiddler out of business, but in Wieniawski's day good Strads and Amatis were still in the market for under $1,000.

A close friend and colleague was Nicolai Rubinstein, brother of the great pianist Anton. The card shown indicates that they were together in Greece. Later they visited the United States for a coast-to-coast tour.

N. Rubinstein

HENRI WIENIAWSKI

Vous prient de dîner avec eux avant leur départ définitif Vendredi 8 heures Café riche sans façons un mot de réponse

24, rue de Florence — BRUXELLES

Wieniawski's dissipations brought on a heart condition which caused his death at the early age of 45. Once in Berlin he succumbed to an attack in the midst of a concert. Joachim happened to be in the audience and finished the concert for him. Thereafter Wieniawski played his concerts seated in a chair.

In an extract from the letter below, Prof. Wieniawski assures his correspondent that his *Variation* is quite playable "except for the passage which becomes especially difficult at the 4th beat . . . as for the cadenza, mark it with some naturals. The passage in double staccato appears to me to be too risky. Of any 100 violinists, two would play it badly, the other 98 wouldn't even try it."

PABLO SARASATE
(1844-1908)

18-11 — 1904

SARASATE   2524.B

Pablo de Sarasate

Most famous Spanish violinist was the great virtuoso Pablo de Sarasate, who will be remembered for his Gypsy airs and arrangements of Spanish dances.

Sarasate had no wives as he never married, and he had no pupils as he never gave lessons. His entire time and energy were devoted to his concerts and his favorite topic was the triumph of his most recent appearance. Evidence substantiating this observation is found in many letters written to his mother.

This player's hands were said to be too small to attempt technical feats of the sort performed by Paganini. Nevertheless he played the first performance of Lalo's *Symphony Espagnole* which was written for him. He likewise played the first performance of Bruch's D minor concerto, also dedicated to him. Sarasate's programs gave great pleasure because of the sweetness and purity of his tone, his perfect intonation and the scrupulous neatness of his playing.

Queen Maria Christina personally invested him with the Grand Cross of Isabel la Catolica which gave him the title "Excellency" as used on the card below.

AUGUST WILHELMJ

(1845-1908)

Air for G String _____ Bach-Wilhelmj

This line on violin recital programs is a familiar one, because some 100 years ago Wilhelmj lifted a flute passage from Bach's concerto in D minor and transcribed it for a violin solo. This displeased some Bach purists who faulted him for presumption. However, from a fiddler's point of view, Wilhelmj's nerve turned out to be a good idea. This noble air has been programmed, encored and recorded repeatedly, so that millions of music lovers are familiar with it who might never have heard it in Bach's context.

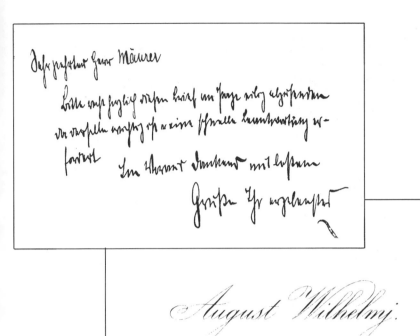

Wilhelmj was a German-born musician full of energy and industry. He was a rabid Wagnerite, held in esteem by the composer who induced him to organize the original Bayreuth orchestra in 1876, of which he was concertmaster. He also contrived to get Wagner to visit London, where Wilhelmj was well established as an important teacher.

Träume .... Wagner-Wilhelmj

Here is another line sometimes found on programs and Wilhelmj's transcription of Wagner's lovely song had the composer's blessing. The two pieces referred to have thus secured for Wilhelmj a tiny bit of violin immortality.

In 1878 this artist embarked on a world tour which included New York City where the photo opposite was taken.

Eugéne Ysaye

EUGENE YSAYE (1858-1931)

The Old Lion of violinists was Ysaye, whose bearing was as regal as was his head leonine. This great Belgian lived a long life of meaningful performance as virtuoso, chamber music player and conductor. His career included many visits to America, and a four-year residence in Cincinnati, Ohio, where he was conductor of that city's symphony orchestra. Other orchestras sought him as soloist; he toured jointly with Mischa Elman as a rare two-violin attraction. At home the Queen named a violin contest in his honor.

Ysaye enjoyed the friendship of many contemporary composers and had an unusual number of works dedicated to him. Fauré dedicated a sonata to him and so did César Franck (his greatest). Chausson's famous *Poème* was written for Ysaye, and other composers who favored him were Debussy, Saint-Saens, d'Indy, Dukas, Pierné, Duparc and many more.

On the facing page this beloved character addresses his violin repair man in a novel message for a visiting card.

28

Bravö. mes violons sont
admirablement répa ès
et je vous félicite. .

EUGÈNE YSAŸE

Maître de Chapelle de S.M. le Roi des Belges.

Je viendrai voir les
archets sitôt que
je trouverai le temps

En ce qui concerne l'assurance
vous avez raison, mais
comme il s'agirait de 4.000 L
et que les temps sont durs
j'attendrai encore d'abord.
d'autant que je ne voyage pas
maintenant. à vous. Eug. Ysaÿe

"Bravo! My violins perfectly repaired and I congratu-
late you. I shall come to see the bows as soon as I
have time. As to insurance, you are right, but it would
cost 4,000 L and times are hard; I shall still wait.
Especially since I do not travel any more now."

Ysaye was 22 years the senior of Jacques Thibaud, and Thibaud was often spoken of as his protegé. These two men shown opposite were kindred musical souls and close friends.

Now another great friend of the Lion was the pianist Raoul Pugno (1852-1914), Mozart specialist, teacher at the conservatory and Ysaye's favorite sonata partner. Below they are shown at one of many joint recitals given at the Salle Pleyel in Paris.

YSAYE et PUGNO à la Salle Pleyel

"Aren't we cute?" Pugno remarks to a lady friend to whom he also sends kisses. The jocular question refers to the weight of the sonata pair — surely the heftiest musicians of their era, who must have tipped the beam well over 400 lb. between them.

JENÖ HUBAY
(1858-1937)

Born in Budapest where his father, Karl Hubay (Huber) was violin professor at the conservatory, young Jenö showed the precocity of a prodigy and at age 13 was recipient of a state scholarship which permitted five years of study under Joachim at the Berlin Hochschule.

For six years thereafter he concertized widely throughout Europe, and when only 24 years of age was invited to occupy the violin chair at the Brussels conservatory. Four years later, on the death of his father, he returned to Budapest to take his father's place at the conservatory and there became one of the most famous teachers of violin, a host of exceptional graduates attesting to his prominence in this field. Most famous of his pupils was Joseph Szigeti, and others were Franz von Vecsey, Erna Rubinstein, Steffi Geier, Eddy Brown and Jelly d'Aranyi.

In 1907 he was knighted and could if he wished call himself *Hubay von Szalatna*.

Hubay composed five operas all of which were produced in Budapest. On the facing page are two bars in his hand from his third opera *A Cremonai Hegedus* based on the Francois Coppée play *Le Luthier de Crémone*.

33

FRITZ KREISLER
(1875-1962)

Few violinists have enjoyed the success of Fritz Kreisler, the most popular and beloved favorite, who toured the United States for 45 years and earned millions from concert receipts and royalties from recordings and his own compositions.

Violinists are not by tradition or inclination likely to be warriors. Few have served in the armed forces and those were wisely assigned to Special Services, playing for camps, hospitals and charity drives. There is one notable exception. Fritz Kreisler was the only violinist to serve in actual combat. In 1914 as an officer in the Austrian army he was twice wounded in action, and mustered out of service. Wounded veterans are considered heroes by the public and Kreisler's return to the concert stage found him to be a sell-out drawing card.

There is a phenomenon of the concert hall often described by critics as a *standing ovation*. It is a demonstration which usually occurs at the close of a performance when most of the audience is standing anyway, about to go home. In Kreisler's case he was frequently given such a reception before he played a note. It was the personal magnetism of the man, the aura of greatness about him, unseen but deeply felt, which caused an audience to rise at his entrance and applaud, a real *standing ovation,* a tribute to the presence of a great man.

The violin recital literature always needs short pieces for the second half of the program and for encores. Kreisler composed 16 such pieces, but believed that if he published them in his own name few rival violinists would use them. So he pretended they were arrangements of obscure compositions by ancient composers such as Corelli, Pugnani, Tartini, Couperin, Porpora, Cartier, Vivaldi, et al.

This hoax was unmasked in 1935 by Olin Downes in a front page story in the *New York Times.* Kreisler admitted these pseudo-classical works were his own, and also three supposedly "old Viennese dances" which were actually new pieces by himself, to wit: *Liebesfreud, Liebeslied,* and *Schon Rosmarin.*

Two of his pet compositions, *Caprice Viennois* and *Tambourin Chinois,* Kreisler never shared with the ancients. They are definitely "in the style of Kreisler." The list that he made of popular tunes from operas and piano selections and rearrangements of violin pieces by others is very long and very fine.

Kreisler was particularly intrigued by cadenzas. A cadenza is a florid interlude in a concerto where the soloist is given a chance to show off his technical fireworks. Kreisler composed three cadenzas for the Beethoven concerto Op. 61; three each for Mozart's concertos No. 3 and 4 and two for No. 5; two for Viotti's concerto Op. 22 and one for the Brahms concerto. As these cadenzas are interpolations interrupting the musical swing of the concerto as much as two or three minutes, they have to be good, and Kreisler's are great.

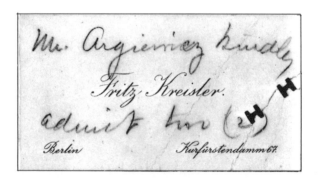

Kreisler stated positively that he not only did not own a visiting card, he never had used one. When confronted with the above item he was amazed. This card was used as a pass to a recital in Carnegie Hall, New York City. The H punch marks signify that Heck Brothers, then Carnegie boxoffice treasurers, honored the pass.

Picture below shows Lt. Kreisler in Vienna before leaving for the front August, 1914. He is with his American wife Harriet, daughter of George P. Lies, a New York tobacco merchant. Right: Up front a few days before being wounded in action at Lemberg (September, 1914).

When Kreisler retired in 1955 he gave the Library of Congress, Washington, the MSS of many of his compositions. On previous occasions he had presented the Library with the original MS of Brahms' violin concerto (full score) and also the original MS of Chausson's *Poème*. This work was dedicated to Ysaye and the composer gave him the MS which he in turn left to Kreisler in his will. In 1952 Kreisler also gave the Library his magnificent violin, a 1733 Guarneri del Gesu.

JAN KUBELIK
(1880-1940)

JAN KUBELIK & HIS WIFE
(COUNTESS CSAKY SZELL.)

The interesting photograph shown above occasions
a comment non-violinistic. When a girl marries a count,
she becomes a countess. Now when a man marries a countess, shouldn't he become a count? Jan Kubelik, renowned
Czech virtuoso, married an Hungarian noblewoman who
went by the name of the Countess Csaky Czell. However,
as Mrs. Kubelik she was mother of five daughters and three
sons, one of the latter being Rafael, successful conductor
of orchestras and operas.

Rafael Kubelik, the conductor, has identified the bar
above as the opening theme of his father's Second Violin
Concerto in D major.

Now there is yet another peculiarity in the case of this
fiddler, best known pupil of Otakar Sevcik and world-wide
celebrity. The Czechs are great for issuing postage stamps
in honor of musicians, including violinists. In fact they have
more violinists on stamps than any other nation* — no less
than five: Slavik (died young); Laub (highly rated in his
era); Sevcik (famous teacher); Suk (quartet player, composer and son-in-law of Dvorak); Ondricek (world traveler,
visited America). But for their star recitalist and most
famous virtuoso Jan Kubelik, there is no stamp! Very odd!

---

* Violinists on stamps: Germany: Spohr and Joachim; Belgium: Vieuxtemps
and Ysaye; Italy: Corelli; Poland: Wieniawski; Austria: Schrammel; Ru-
mania: Enesco; Bolivia: Laredo.

JACQUES THIBAUD
(1880-1953)

Ordinarily a string player does not partake of athletic games, fearing to stiffen his fingers. An exception would be the dapper French fiddler Jacques Thibaud, who had a theory that musicians were too precious about their persons, which denied them the pleasures of sport. To prove his point he took up golf, and vacationed at St. Jean de Luz in southwest France where he tried his skill on a flat links of rugged terrain.

As a concession to his occupation, he wore full-fingered gloves on both hands, and to avoid jarring his wrists he was careful to take no divots. Thus he used woods on all long shots and chipped all his short irons. Under the tutelage of the pro shown, he played a nice fiddler's game in the low nineties.

Mille fois merci, cher ami.

JACQUES THIBAUD

This violinist also had a theory about the way concerted music should be played. He prized spontaneity above perfection and he held that too much practice detracted from the fun and excitement of collaboration. In spite of this theory (not shared, for instance, by Pablo Casals), Thibaud held his position in the great piano trios of which Casals was cellist and Cortot pianist in Europe and Harold Bauer pianist in North America. In fact his suave and elegant tone was a decided asset to these ensembles which had a wide vogue some 50 years ago.

GEORGES ENESCO
(1881-1955)

Greatest Rumanian musician of this century, Enesco was a violin virtuoso, a conductor, a considerable composer, a pedagogue (one of his pupils was Yehudi Menuhin) and a musical *savant*. The term "savant" is a kind of honorary title, an appellation bestowed by friends or critics on a man who is not only expert in his specialty but is learned in all the arts and humanities. Such a man was Enesco.

Les Jeunesses Musicales de France was the name of a young peoples' musical society in Paris which asked Enesco to contribute a letter to their journal. He responded with an eloquent tribute to music which he termed a powerful solace and a great hope, and having a social and moral mission:

"In such a troubled period as the present, music has a higher function than just to occupy one's spare time. It will be an enchanted universe where the tribulations of life do not enter, and where your dreams can find a refuge. It will bring to you those priceless gifts — serenity of mind and forgetfulness of the cruelty of men.

"He who asserts this has been severely tested by events, but still gives thanks for the purified air brought to him by his art. Your generation fulfills wishes secretly formed by ours. Courage! Give yourselves to music without restraint: it will reward your trust!" (October 1948)

While Enesco is now a national hero in his homeland, with memorial stamps issued in his honor, monuments erected and monographs written, his last days were unhappy, with failing health and straitened finances.

The above card written in Rumanian is addressed to
Eduard Candella, an early teacher of Enesco, who first
heard him play at age of five years. Note interesting Rumanian spelling of Enesco's name.

PAUL KLEE
(1879-1940)

As a youth it was a toss-up with Paul Klee whether he would undertake a career as violinist or as painter; he had an unusual and precocious talent for either. Once, playing in the Berne (Switzerland) Orchestra, the concertmaster became ill and the conductor requested Paul, aged 15, to take his place. It is therefore possible to state that no violinist in this book could paint a picture as well as Klee could play the fiddle.

Klee's favorite relaxation was quartet playing and he always played with professionals. When he couldn't get the right ensemble together for a session of Beethoven or Mozart quartets, he could always play sonatas with his wife, Lily, a professional piano teacher.

Of Klee's giant oeuvre of some 9,000 pieces, 5,000 were drawings. Not included in this number is the 5,001st, his only drawing of a violin reproduced herewith. It is a postscript to a letter.

Also of interest is Klee's visiting card, containing on its verso a motto for collectors: "Collecting for the love of it and from a lofty motive is a good thing."

Paul Klee's love of music, his wide acquaintance with its literature, his continuous participation in top-level music making, had a profound effect on his painting and helped to make him one of the greatest artists of this century.

Paul Klee

Sammeln aus Liebe und in Bezug auf das Geistige ist eine gute Sache

Klee

ALBERT SPALDING
(1888-1953)

Drawn by Violet Oakley, 1928

Scion of the great sports equipment company founded by his uncle, A. G. Spalding, Albert Spalding passed up a commercial career to become a successful concert violinist. Gently reared in Florence, Italy, where his family wintered, he grew up in an ambience of culture. Never a college student, he had that larger education of a world traveler, with fluency in three languages and graduate training from the best professors in his chosen specialty.

His proficient knowledge of the Italian language was of use to his country in two wars. In World War I he enlisted, was commissioned and served in Italy on the staff of Capt. Fiorella LaGuardia, the only man ever to call him "Al." In World War II after the Allies landed in Italy his patrician speech was broadcast daily with propaganda messages from southern to northern Italy.

While Jacques Thibaud blazed an athlete's trail among violinists as a golfer, Spalding was an adept at tennis. Fiddlers really do not have much time for outdoor games, but

46

one summer when the Spaldings lived in Gt. Barrington, Mass., Albert was actually champion of the local country club.

Spalding is the only violinist ever listed in the *Social Register*, and he moved in the top social circles of the U.S. and Europe. All of the leading instrumentalists of his day were friends, and so were writers, diplomats and socialites.

When Spalding returned from his stint in the second war, his broadcasting experience stood him in good stead, as he was engaged on a popular hour as MC and played one violin selection on each show. Thus he was on the air weekly for two years, being the only classical violinist to experience such exposure, and no other fiddler has had a like engagement since.

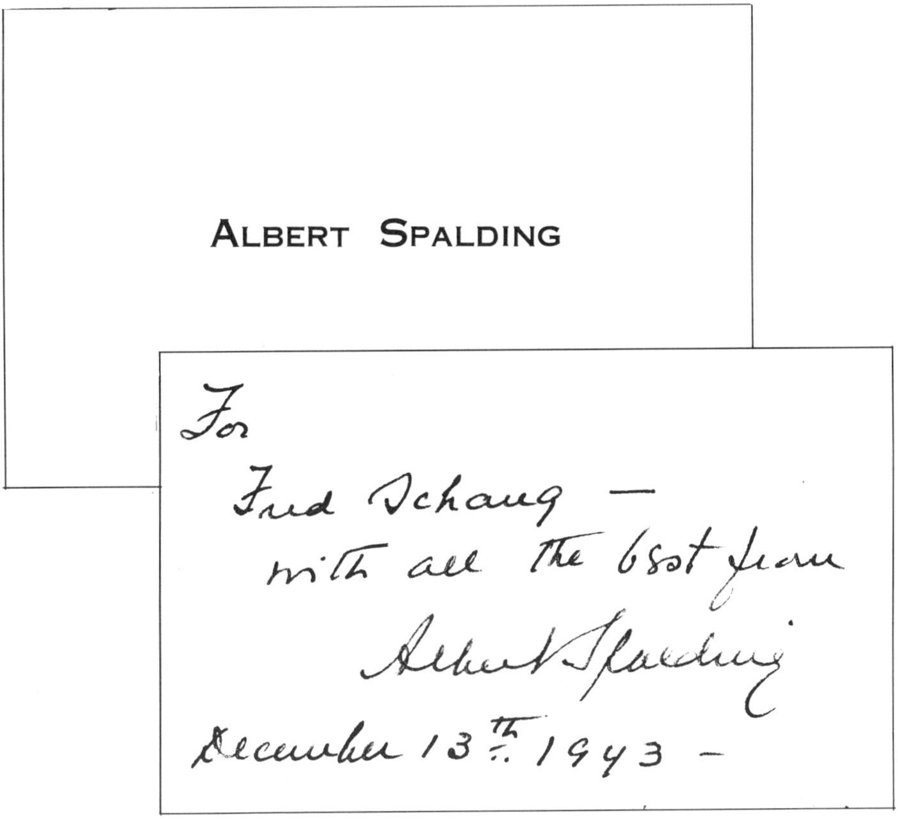

ALBERT SPALDING

For

Fred Schang —
with all the best from

Albert Spalding

December 13th 1943 —

**MISCHA
ELMAN**
(1891-1967)

Mischa Elman was a pioneer recitalist and first violinist to sell a gold record (*Humoreske* of Dvorak). He had
already banked a fortune before the advent of Kreisler and
Heifetz as rival drawing cards. When they surged forward
in the public favor, Elman dropped back to third place, still
a very nice living, but not what Elman was accustomed to.

The profession of violin soloist owes Elman a debt of
gratitude for his early work in grass-roots areas. Years before the organized audience movement developed musical
taste in small localities, Mischa Elman had been the first
and often the only musical artist ever heard in such spots.

This came about because Elman detested hanging
around in hotels between dates. Supposing he were booked
for full fee engagements in New Orleans on Monday and
St. Louis the following Sunday. He directed his management to arrange percentage contracts with theatres or halls

in towns enroute such as Clarksdale, Vicksburg, Hattiesburg, Oxford. As he travelled with an accompanist and manager both engaged by the week, there was hardly any extra expense to play these little dates, and Elman really enjoyed them. He marveled that the audiences, however small, were there at all, and he played his full programs for them, including encores.

Once playing an early December date in Fargo, N.D., a blinding blizzard blew in from the north. The audience had difficulty in reaching the hall, and the heating pipes froze, so Elman had to play the concert in a fur coat and hat. At the close of the concert a couple arrived covered with snow. They had been 13 hours en route from Minot, had encountered heavy drifts and bitter cold. Although Elman was in bad humor because of impossible local conditions, he was greatly impressed by the worse fortune of this couple. He invited them to his hotel for the night and the next morning in the hotel ballroom he played for them his entire program.

Much has been written of Elman's magnificent tone which was indeed exceptional and individual. No scratchy or tentative sounds ever emanated from Elman's Strad. His G string often sounded like a cello. His notes were broad and true, full of sonority and sheen, with enormous volume if appropriate.

yours truly

Mischa Elman

april 20/1946

Once when Elman was soloist at an outdoor concert in Ebbetts Field, Brooklyn, he was induced to put on a Dodger shirt and pose with Jackie Robinson.

Now in Elman's hey-day, the twenties, there existed in Greater New York City a violin public unequalled anywhere before or since. For this was an era of Jewish immigration, and to serve these hundred-thousands there were six Jewish newspapers with a daily circulation of nearly a million. Readers of these papers loved the violin and were the nucleus of huge audiences which assembled Sunday nights in the New York Hippodrome, a vast theatre seating 6,000 with an additional 1,500 on the stage. Mischa Elman was the favorite violinist of this audience, and no wonder, for in this great hall his mighty tones were heard in its furthest extremities.

Following the example of other violinists of the past who had organized string quartets (Joachim, Rosé, Ysaye), Elman tried this idea out for a time with indifferent success. Actually he was too dominant a player for a quartet and financially he was worth more in recital than accompanied by three other salaries. It was after hearing a concert by this quartet that Harry Zelzer, the Chicago concert tycoon, made the historic observation: "Good music is not as bad as it sounds."

Handsome youth was Jascha Heifetz, shown here with his celebrated teacher Prof. Leopold Auer (1845-1930), who was also teacher of Mischa Elman, Efrem Zimbalist and others.

JASCHA HEIFETZ

The Golden Age of violin playing must be those years when Kreisler, Heifetz and Elman were all in the field and all playing their best. Paced by this trio were a host of outstanding performers — Menuhin, Francescatti, Milstein, Morini, Spivakovsky, Goldberg, Ricci, Spalding, Glenn, in all a terrific lineup, not likely to be equalled in the near future.

An 18-carat contributor to this golden age was Jascha Heifetz, a superlative performer and a perfectionist in a class by himself. Since his taste was faultless and his playing flawless, the only possible reservations that could be made referred to his austere countenance. On stage Heifetz did not smile, in fact he presented a neutral demeanor, as if to discourage the audience from any thought other than the music being played. Once when he gave a recital before a ladies music club, one of the members was heard to remark: "He plays so beautifully, why is he so glum about it?"

Late in his career his health forbade travel, so his efforts have been devoted to teaching and trio playing with Piatigorsky and Pennario, fellow Californians. He also made a TV documentary in which he is seen to smile several times, and to play a sharp game of ping-pong.

ZINO FRANCESCATTI
(1904-   )

When Zino Francescatti made his American debut with the New York Philharmonic-Symphony in 1939, he played the Paganini concerto using the original edition which had been a gift from his father, René, who was his teacher. The elder Francescatti had in turn received this edition from his teacher, Camillo Savori (1815-1894), Paganini's favorite and most famous pupil. By this succession of incidents a direct connection between Paganini and Francescatti is established.

While some violinists today disdain the experience to be obtained as a member of a symphony orchestra, fearing to subordinate their personalities, many virtuosos of the past, and some of the present, have found such a stint a useful part of their training. Old timers such as Joachim, Wilhelmj, Ysaye, Busch, Thibaud and current virtuosos such as Spivakovsky, Goldberg and Francescatti have all in their youth welcomed such an opportunity, and one of the reasons Francescatti is an outstanding choice of conductors as soloist is their knowledge of his special understanding and skill because of this early experience.

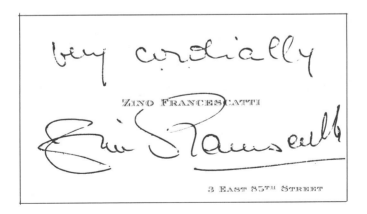

55

ERICA MORINI
(1906-   )

In 1920 when the impresario F. C. Coppicus decided to engage Erica Morini for an American tour, he knew very well that there was a prejudice against female violin soloists, particularly on the part of orchestras, which always seemed to hire men for solo jobs. However, he believed that the Morini girl, at the age of 15 already a seasoned and veteran prodigy (she had been playing in public for six years), would be the one to break down this prejudice and blaze a new trail for female fiddlers.

Erica Morini

*To my first american
maufti with kind
regards
Erica Morini*

So with eyes wide open to the financial perils involved, he planned an orchestral debut for the young Austrian virtuosa. He engaged an orchestra with Artur Bodanzky as conductor, and presented Miss Morini in a program of three concertos, an unheard of gamble in those days. Thus Erica played in one session, concertos by Mozart, Vieuxtemps and Mendelssohn, on an historic occasion which at once established her as a legitimate competitor in the stag world of violin-playing brethren.

That was over 50 years ago. In that half-century Erica Morini has played many, many orchestral engagements and has come to be acknowledged the greatest living woman violinist. And what is more, she is probably the greatest ever!

TOSSY SPIVAKOVSKY (1907-   )

In the annals of American violinists, Tossy Spivakovsky will go down as the man who introduced two very difficult violin concertos, those of Bela Bartok and Roger Sessions.

He will also be remembered for an individual way of holding the violin and bowing it, devised by him to facilitate the playing of polyphonic chords in the six unaccompanied sonatas and partitas of J. S. Bach. His scholarship, research and conclusions on the three and four-note chords in these works may well turn out to be his most important contribution to the lore of violin-playing.

Now it seems that in these six pieces of Bach there are by Spivakovsky's count 1290 polyphonic chords. It is obvious that to play an unbroken four-note chord on the violin is a feat demanding virtuoso technique. By many violinists it was considered an impossibility. This school solved the problem by arpeggiating all four-note chords and many three-note chords.

Such a solution was unsatisfactory to Spivakovsky. He held that since Bach was himself a violinist, and a most meticulous penman, he would not write down chords which were unplayable. Nor would he mark certain chords "arpeggio" if he did not mean that those not so marked were to be played unbroken.

To Fred

TOSSY SPIVAKOVSKY

with affection

Tossy

Equipment was the solution of the problem. An arched bow capable of straddling the four strings permits a proficient technician to sound a legato unbroken four-note chord. Spivakovsky declares he is able to play 1288 out of 1290 polyphonic chords as written by Bach. In the two "unplayable" chords he says Bach made slips of the pen and the chords are easily rectified in the context.

Why all this pother about a matter of concern to only a handful of fiddlers? Not at all! Knowledge of Bach's *oeuvre* is mandatory for all violinists and found therein is the *Chaconne,* conceded to be the greatest single piece of music ever written for the violin. It is important that this masterpiece be played as intended by the composer and not distorted for the convenience of performers.

So thank you, Mr. Spivakovsky. In fact, hurray for Tossy! Let us hope he has settled this matter for good and all.

The case for arpeggiation is stated in *The History of Violin Playing from its Origin to 1761* by David D. Boyden. London, Oxford University Press, 1965. The masterful rebuttal is found in *Polyphony in Bach's Works for Solo Violin* by Tossy Spivakovsky The Music Review Vol. 28 No. 4, November 1967.

Arched bow referred to made by Knud Vestergaard, Viby, Jutland (Denmark).

DAVID OISTRAKH
(1908-1974)

"To my dear friend Fred Schang with much gratitude for
his warm attentiveness to me" — New York, 16 Jan. 1960

In the autumn of 1954 a note in the papers stated that
the USSR had joined UNICEF. Now this United Nations
organization was 10 years old and the Soviets could have
joined it at anytime. A New York concert manager correctly
interpreted this note to mean that the Russians were rolling
back the iron curtain and were ripe for a cultural exchange.
To this certain manager *cultural exchange* meant at long
last a chance to get the Soviets' great violinist, David
Oistrakh, for the first visit to America of any Soviet artist
since the revolution.

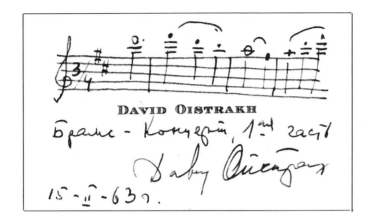

DAVID OISTRAKH

Брамс - Концерт, 1-й часть

15 - II - 63 г.

A call to the Soviet Embassy in Washington confirmed that this possibility was indeed a fact and within a week a contract was arranged to bring the great star to the U.S. He arrived in the fall of 1955 and proved to be an overwhelming drawing card. Two recitals were announced for Carnegie Hall in the Sunday papers and on Monday morning an extraordinary crowd lined up four abreast from the box office around the building to the middle of 56th Street, and both concerts were sold out by noon.

Artistically Oistrakh was an immediate success playing with the easy mastery of genius, and he was compared only to Paganini and Heifetz. Off stage his modesty and friendliness made him the most popular of Soviet visitors.

Давид Фёдорович
Ойстрах

профессор Московской Государственной
Консерватории

Top card shows bars from Brahms' violin concerto. Bottom card in Cyrillic script gives academic title, Professor at Moscow State Conservatory.

61

Rehearsing with Philadelphia Orchestra, Ormandy conducting.

When Oistrakh arrived the schedule for the Philadelphia Orchestra was complete. However, Eugene Ormandy was determined that the newcomer would make his first orchestral appearance with his band, so he juggled dates and soloists to make a suitable opening, and the Philadelphia Orchestra had the satisfaction of making this first presentation.

Some days later Oistrakh remarked that he had brought with him the full score and parts of a new violin concerto by Shostakovitch. The New York Philharmonic cleared the decks for this work's debut, which took place in December, Mitropoulos conducting. Oistrakh's playing created a sensation and the work was a *tour de force*.

The sad news of Oistrakh's death in Amsterdam, October 1974, was a first page story in the New York Times, whose critic Harold Schonberg wrote: "His playing had an inner sweetness that was a reflection of the man himself."

Rare photo of David Oistrakh circa 1945, with his prodigy son Igor. Latter has toured widely and is also a professor in the State Conservatory of Music, Moscow.

**SZYMON
GOLDBERG
(1 9 0 9 -   )**

Although a consummate violinist with a style and re-
finement all his own, Szymon Goldberg must be appraised
for his all-around erudition and his ability to function at a
top level in various musical capacities.

As a boy prodigy in his native Poland, he moved to
Germany for more advanced study, progressed so rapidly
that at age 16 he was concert master of the Dresden Symphony, and at 20 of the Berlin Philharmonic, Furtwängler
conducting, a post he held for four years. In between times
he concertized in a famous trio, the other two members being Emanuel Feuerman, cellist, and Paul Hindemith, pianist.

World War II found him on a far eastern tour where
the Japanese interned him in Java for two and a half years.
In some miraculous way he managed to preserve his violin.

Coming to the United States, he gave a notable recital
at Carnegie Hall, New York City, remembered to this day
by experts as an outstanding event. Now his inspirational
powers as a teacher were enlisted by the Aspen (Colo.)
Festival, where he remained for ten summers, founding the
Festival Quartet with Victor Babin, William Primrose and
Nicolai Graudan. This peerless group toured for seven years.

SZYMON GOLDBERG

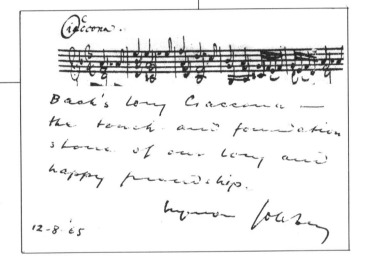

Ciaccona.

Bach's long Ciaccona — the touch and foundation stone of our long and happy friendship.

Szymon Goldberg

12-8-65

Summoned to Amsterdam by the Netherlands Chamber Orchestra as conductor and solo violinist, Goldberg has brought this fine ensemble to a position of world prominence.

While Mozart lovers everywhere belong to a secret cult, each member of which believes he is the only one who really understands Mozart, they all step aside to listen to Szymon Goldberg, master interpreter of the genius of the Salzkammergut. Last winter at the Queen Elizabeth Hall, London, with the Rumanian pianist Radu Lupu, he took part in four sold out concerts in which 16 Mozart sonatas were presented.

YEHUDI MENUHIN
(1916-   )

Yehudi Menuhin, the first American-born violin prodigy, grew up to be more than a leading virtuoso; he became a dynamic musical force, not only in his native land, but also in several European countries, notably England and Switzerland. Considering his wide knowledge, his varied contributions and his world outlook, Yehudi Menuhin is the musical savant of his era.

This view is supported by the many honors bestowed upon him. He has received no less than ten honorary doctorates from universities which include titles from London, Oxford, Cambridge and St. Andrews. In 1970 he accepted the highest honor India can grant, the Jawaharlal Nehru Award for International Understanding. Other decorations from Gt. Britain, France, Greece, Belgium and Holland have crowded his lapel with ribbons, in recognition of his life-long efforts in musical and humanitarian fields.

In 1972 a collection of his essays on music and life called *Theme and Variations* was widely acclaimed. The New York Times declared "the ultimate message of this extraordinary American violinist is one of hope."

Menuhin does not presently use visiting cards. Like Kreisler before him, he stated that he had never owned one, and was very surprised when confronted with the above card. Writing spells out his name in Hebrew.

RUGGIERO RICCI (1920-   )

Toujours en voyage is the lot of the violin virtuoso, but it's a way to see the world and to meet people. There is just no fiddler living or dead whose travels can equal those of Ruggiero Ricci. A truly international concert artist, aside from annual tours in North America and Europe, Ricci had gone round-the-world three times; he has visited Russia and Australia three times, he has toured South Africa four times and made nine trips to South America.

Furthermore, as a musical ambassador under State Department auspices, he has been to remote parts of Africa such as Bengali and Ghana. And when a young man he did a tour of duty for the Army Air Forces that carried him everywhere.

During this stint he was called upon often to entertain in army camps where there was no accompanist, no piano or both. He was forced to fall back on the unaccompanied violin and started at this early age to develop his remarkable ability to hold an audience's attention in unaccompanied pieces for the violin. Foundation for such programs is of course the Bach oeuvre and the 24 Paganini *Caprices*. But Ricci has a flock of other pieces, including works by Hindemith and Bartok.

A logical consequence of his mastery of this literature led him to give recitals in London and New York recently where there was no piano on the stage. Audience and critics alike were enchanted with the program which included Prokofieff's *Sonata for two violins,* Villa-Lobos' *Suite for Voice and Violin* and Saint-Saens *Fantaisie for Violin and Harp.*

Card is for Swiss residence used when working in Europe. Artist also has abodes in New York and Mexico Cities, and at Bloomington, Ind., when teaching at the University there.

ISAAC STERN
(1 9 2 0 -   )

Indefatigable world traveler and interested participant in diverse musical activities, Isaac Stern is a most important performing fiddler and leader of the current generation of players.

In 1960 when Carnegie Hall was about to be sold for another highrise, Stern intervened, succeeded in getting the City of New York to buy Carnegie and lease it to a non-profit organization of which he is still president. The availability of this great concert hall with its superior acoustics is of utmost importance to the city's musical life and has been for years the auditorium used by visiting symphony orchestras from Europe and other cities in North America.

In addition to a full schedule of recitals and orchestral appearances Stern finds the time to play trio concerts with Eugene Istomen and Leonard Rose. It is the best trio available since Bauer, Casals and Thibaud toured in the twenties.

Stern's boundless energy permits him to participate in the America-Israel Cultural Foundation, the National Council on the Arts, the Kennedy Center, etc. In an odd moment he even dashed off a violin sound track for the musical *Fiddler on the Roof.*

To Fred Schang —
who, despite being a

ISAAC STERN

manager, likes music
so.

Isaac Stern

Feb. 10-1966

CARROLL GLENN
(1 9 2 4 -   )

Carroll Glenn is without challenge the greatest native-born woman violinist, and let's have no nonsense about the way to spell "Carroll", it's with two r's and two l's, for she is a direct descendant of a Signer,* Charles Carroll of Carrollton, Maryland, a town which is still in existence with a zip code of 21025.

---

*Q. What Signer of the Declaration of Independence was also a fiddler? A. Thomas Jefferson — he owned an Amati.

To Freddie –

Miss Carroll Glenn

With love and
concern remembrances
Glenn chee—

This fiery virtuosa gets big tones out of her "Lord Walton" Guarneri and she is a wizard playing concertos suited to her temperament, as for instance the concerto of Aram Khatchaturian. She also made it her business to introduce contemporary concertos, those by Gail Kubick, Harold Morris and most recently Andrew Imbrie.

With her husband, the fine pianist Eugene List, she played the world premier of a Franz Liszt sonata at the Library of Congress, the MS of which just turned up after all these years. This attractive pair have also presented sonatas by the contemporaries Manual Rosenthal, Anis Fuleihan and Paul Nordoff.

A high spot in the careers of these artists was when the U.S. State Department sent them on a good will tour of the far east. There is just no couple in the concert world so suited for such a mission, which earned them high praises everywhere.

The Lists reside in Rochester, N.Y., as both are members of the faculty of the Eastman School of Music. Summertime finds them with their daughters Allison and Rachel at their home in Manchester, Vermont.

PRODIGIES
and
PARENTS

A PHENOMENON peculiar to the violinist's profession is the early age at which children are committed to such a career. In fact every artist listed in this book started out as a child prodigy.

It seems that no age is too tender to implant a perfect sense of intonation in the subconscious of a future fiddler. And half and three-quarter size instruments are available so that immature fingers can nevertheless develop digital facility.

According to the biographies of these musical whiz kids they start out playing at the age of five, often with father as first teacher. A few years later they are winning prizes at conservatories. Not long after they make their debuts in public, at least one critic will dub them "Second Paganinis" and sometimes royalty or a rich patron will present them with a Strad.

Now whenever there are minor children earning money on the stage, parents will be found in the dressing room. In former days the behavior of certain indigent parents smacked of child labor, but latterly parents are more enlightened, limit the public appearances of their geniuses, do not permit the career to interfere with a general education and reasonable recreation.

Drawn by Conrado Massaguer

Said Poppa Elman to Poppa Menuhin:
"How is your boy Yehudi doin'?"
"It's immortal the way he weaves a spell, man!"
Said Poppa Menuhin to Poppa Elman.

One blessing comes to the boy violin prodigy. He does not have to face a youth's dilemma, how to decide what career to pursue. Almost from the time he's weaned, he knows he is going to fiddle for a living.

An interesting father of a prodigy was old man Elman, sire of Mischa, and definitely a character in his own right. He had his hands full keeping up with the receipts which rivals were drawing in Boston, Toronto, Tchick-a-go, Washington and other key cities. He personally attended important concerts given by his son. In his fur-collared coat he hung around the lobby watching the customers flock in, and greeting the critics, hoping to pick up some tip or morsel of useful information. At curtain time he drifted back stage and took charge of the fiddle case with the extra bows. At the concert's conclusion he minded the violin and kept an eye on the coats and hats while youngsters came back stage to get their programs autographed. Mischa was very fond of his father and listened with great patience to an endless stream of reports. If the concert was at Carnegie Hall, New York City, then father and son, accompanist and manager, and a number of Russian-speaking buddies dropped into the Russian Tea Room next door for a discussion of highlights of the concert and a ration of tea and blintzes.

If the concert were in Chicago, then impresario Harry Zelzer, the midwestern concert czar, would throw a party at the Yar restaurant where good borscht was obtainable. Zelzer engaged Elman annually at a special fee of $1,000. One year Elman changed managers, and the new manager raised the fee to $2,000, so Zelzer didn't book him. Mischa was upset to learn there was no Chicago concert. He knew that Zelzer liked his father so he sent him to find out why he had not been engaged. Zelzer was quick to tell old man Elman that $2,000 was too rich for his blood. After futile arguments, finally the old man asked "Don't you have any sentiment?" "Yes," said Zelzer, "but only up to $1,000. Above that figure I have no sentiment."

———

Maud Powell (1868-1920) was a fine American violinist and would have been included in this book had her visiting card been obtainable. As it is, find her photograph as a prodigy aged 13 on page 79.

———

Opposite we have a page photographed from Dr. Boehler's *Schattenrisse*, an album of silhouettes which he compiled for the fun of it. Dr. Boehler was friendly with the musical world of Vienna in the eighteen-nineties. The occasion is an audition of the boy Bronislaw Huberman playing the Brahms violin concerto. Among the listeners, Brahms himself and Bruckner, Kienzl, J. Strauss, Ed. Hanslick et al. Probable date, 1892.

FOUR CELEBRATED PRODIGIES

Fritz Kreisler

Georges Enesco

Mischa Elman

Jascha Heifetz

FOUR AMERICAN-BORN PRODIGIES

Maud Powell

Yehudi Menuhin

Ruggiero Ricci

Carroll Glenn

Elman, Enesco, Heifetz, Spalding, Morini, Francescatti.